is hereby certified as a

Genuine

Article

Presented by:

Date:

genuine

Being real
in an
artificial
world

Stacie Orrico

J. Countryman
Nashville, Tennessee

Photo credits:
Copyright © 2001 Allen Clark @ TIG — Cover and pages 5, 15 ,56
Copyright © 2001 Kristin Barlowe — Front and back covers, front end sheets, pages 3,
        5, 11, 20, 31, 45, 46, 51, 55, 56
Copyright © 2001 Matthew Barnes — Pages 6, 7, 23, 37, 57

Quizzes — Jennifer Case Cortez
J. Countryman® is a trademark of Thomas Nelson Inc.
Designed by Uttley/DouPonce DesignWorks, Sisters, Oregon
Project editor: Jenny Baumgartner
Extreme for Jesus™ Brand Manager: Hayley Morgan
ISBN: 0-8499-9545-0
Printed and bound in the United States of America
www.jcountryman.com

Stacie's Sound

I describe my music as a pop R&B. I like urban R&B music because I think it has this deep sound that pulls at your soul like no other kind of music. I've been influenced by a lot of old music. Some of my favorite older musicians are Ella Fitzgerald, Tony Bennett, and Billie Holiday. My favorite artist is Lauryn Hill. She's definitely got soul, but I listen to all kinds of music—from country to alternative to classical.

The Story Behind the Song "Genuine"

In junior high school, I struggled with fitting in and with finding my place in the world. I couldn't figure out where I belonged, and neither could my friends. We started making bad decisions, and I saw myself doing things I didn't think I would do and saying things I never thought I would say.

Even though I was probably in the "in crowd" at school, I wasn't enjoying it. I was often trying to make peace between people who were upset with each other. But then I'd end up just saying something that would make them feel like they weren't spiritual enough. Even though it wasn't my intention, I made them feel like I thought I was a better Christian.

I've been guilty of that so often. So many times, we think our motives are pure, but they're not. It's okay to tell your friends that they're doing something that they shouldn't be doing, but for me, it came down to criticizing them rather than just loving them and trying to encourage them. Even the things I did that **seemed** good really weren't. I found myself trying to be very nice to people. I thought, *Maybe if I'm sweet, people will think better of me.* But it wasn't totally me. It wasn't even the right motive. It wasn't genuine.

Because of all that was happening, I was confused and frustrated. I got to a point where I just gave up and said, "I don't even care. I don't care what anybody thinks." Then one day, I was at home alone, sitting in my kitchen, and I just started praying, "Lord, I'm so tired of this. I'm so tired of feeling like I'm going to get put down anytime I do something or say something. And I'm tired of my

friends feeling like they have to do all these things to fit in. Help me, Lord."

Then, with God's help, I started to realize that I needed something real—a foundation for life—and I found it in Him. That day, I wrote the song "Genuine." The words helped to express my heart and gave me a new challenge in life.

* This song, my album Genuine, and my whole message is wrapped around the word genuine.

*You're trying so hard to fit in...

It's what He gives — It's who He is — It's what He has — It's what He gives... What He gives is something truthful...

genuine 6

What you need is something genuine.... I go to Him because.... what He has is something genuine.... who He is is someone real....

Life is all about being real, about being happy with who you are. If I could sum it up in just a few words, I would say that I want people to find their identity in Christ; I want them to know how precious they are to God. He thinks we are so amazing! I believe that if we are reminded of that enough, we can change a lot of things. I want others to say, "Wow! God thinks I'm beautiful!"

Stacie Orrico

genuine 7

GENUINE *

GENUINE

I see you passing by – I don't know where – I don't know why . . .
You choose to go the way that you're goin' now
You've been a friend of mine for many years for a long time, but . . .
You just aren't you today, so what's on your mind . . .
You just don't want to speak about it – think about it – be about it . . .
Gotta make yourself aware that you're going' astray . . .
You're trying so hard to fit in

CHORUS:

(What you need is something genuine . . .
What you want is something real . . .
What you need is something truthful . . .
I know you do (3x) 'Cause I need it to . . .
What you need (2x) . . . What you want (2x) . . .
What you need (2x) something genuine)

You cry yourself to sleep – sleep at night but once the night is gone . . .
And you prepare to face a brand new day . . .
You hide yourself behind that mastermind – you're in disguise . . .
It's as if you try to put a mask on your pain
You don't know who you are – what you're about –

Where you are now . . .
You're becoming someone that you don't want to be . . .
You're trying so hard to fit in

CHORUS

He loves you for who you are now and who you will be . . .
Don't fear living in truth there's reality . . .
I don't have all the answers but I know One who does . . .
And I know there's freedom and truth . . .
I go to Him because
(What you need is something genuine . . . I know you do . . .
What you need is something truthful - genuine . . .
What you need (2x) What you want (2x) . . .
What you need (2x) something genuine)
What He has is something genuine . . .
Who He is is someone real . . .
What He gives is something truthful
It's what He has - it's who He is - it's what He gives . . .
And I need Him too . . .
What you need (2x)
I need Him too . . .
What you want (2x) . . . what you need (2x)
What you need (2x) something genuine

Then you will know the truth,

and the truth will make you free.

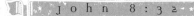

John 8:32

it's all
about being
genuine

What a mystery
I find in the future.

A Singing Baby

I love music. It's always been a part of my life.

I started singing when I was in my crib. My mom says she would come in to my room, and I'd be standing at the side of my crib, singing away. I can't remember a time when music wasn't the center of my life.

I didn't really choose a music career on purpose. I loved singing and everything about music, but I never thought about doing it professionally. Before I was offered a record deal (at age thirteen), I was just worrying about going to junior high and becoming a teenager! But now I can't imagine doing anything else.

I'VE LEARNED THAT WHEN YOU HAVE CHRIST IN THE MIDDLE OF YOUR LIFE, HE'LL TAKE YOU TO AMAZING PLACES. HE GIVES YOU OPPORTUNITIES THAT YOU'VE NEVER DREAMED OF.

My Musical Family

I grew up in a music-filled home. We always have music playing, and we sometimes sing while we are doing the dishes. My dad and my older brother play the guitar. My mom, sister, and I play the piano. It's funny that some people have called us the von Trapp-Orrico family, after the von Trapps in the movie, The Sound of Music. WE HATE THAT. 😊

Stacie's Hobbies

I HAVE THE PRIVILEGE OF LIVING OUT ALL OF MY HOBBIES. SINGING, WRITING, TRAVELING, AND DANCING—I GET TO DO IT ALL.

Becoming A Star

I signed a record deal when I was thirteen. It all started at an event called Seminar in the Rockies, which is an annual Christian music festival in Estes Park, Colorado. When my mom found out that it included a singing competition, she asked me if I wanted to enter it. I had never been in a competition before, but I decided I would try.

I was twelve at the time and I sang with seventy-five teens— ages twelve to eighteen. The other singers were amazing—they seemed like child prodigies! They had been practicing their songs for months, and I'd just picked mine at the last minute. At that point, I panicked and thought, "What am I doing here?!" I'd never been nervous singing in front of people, but I was shaking at the competition.

I sang two songs, one called "Sea of Forgetfulness" by Helen Baylor and "Not Too Far

Me @ Seminar in the Rockies

From Here" by Kim Boyce. Then they announced that I'd won the competition! I was feeling so cool, and just when I thought the excitement was over, Eddie DeGarmo came up and started talking with my family and I about a record deal. (Eddie was one of the judges of the competition, and he was with Forefront Records in Nashville, Tennessee.)

At first I didn't really even know if I wanted to be a professional singer, and I didn't understand the whole music industry. But we slowly eased into it, and now that I look back, I see that it was totally a God thing.

The year I competed was the first time in twenty-six years that they'd lowered the age to twelve for competing. Then God brought Eddie and many other people into my life who helped me take the next steps. God set it all up perfectly—His hand has been on me the whole way.

MY FAVORITE BAND: GOO GOO DOLLS. EVEN THOUGH EVERY ONE OF THEIR SONGS HAS BEEN OVERPLAYED ON THE RADIO, THEY'RE STILL MY FAVORITE BAND.

Staying

Genuine

in the

Music Spotlight

When I meet other teens, a lot of times they'll act strange at first. They don't know what to do, so they wait to see how I will react or how I will deal with their questions. I'll say something like, "Hey, I see you're wearing a soccer jersey," and I'll talk to them about soccer and everyday stuff. Then they warm up quickly. They're like, "Oh, you're real!" It is refreshing to me when people know that I'm no different than they are. It keeps me grounded.

I also am balanced by everybody around me—at home and on the road. They totally treat me like "little fifteen-year-old Stacie." They'll jokingly make fun of me, or they'll tell me, "You carry your own bag!" They're so straight with me. It's awesome.

Sometimes, people from the record label will go out on the road with me. If they don't know me very well, they'll constantly ask, "Do you need something?" They're just trying to take care of me, but it's weird to me to have the special treatment. It makes me wonder, *Have I changed? Or am I putting off this vibe, like, Y'all need to be treatin' me different!* I pray that isn't the case because it's important to me to be genuine.

I want to be genuine so that I'm not hiding any part of me from God or from the people closest to me. I want to stay true to what God has given to me.

I WORKED ON THE ALBUM GENUINE FOR A YEAR AND A HALF, AND I WROTE THREE SONGS ON IT: "GENUINE," "DON'T LOOK AT ME," AND "DEAR FRIEND."

genuine

17

Stacies
favorites

Bible Verse: Psalm 100

Book: Green Eggs and Ham by Dr. Seuss

Celebrity: Lauryn Hill

Recipe: Snickerdoodles, 'cause you get to roll the dough in the cinnamon and sugar

Memory: Jumping in piles of leaves in the fall with my older brother and sister in the backyard when I was little

Color: silver

Song: "Ex-Factor" by Lauryn Hill

Movie: "Sister Act 2" or "While You Were Sleeping" I also love old Cary Grant movies.

Person: My sister Rachel

Animal: Hippo

Plant: Fire and ice roses

Food: Mexican

F.Y.I.– Stacie's Birthday: March 3rd

Genuine

18

My favorites

Bible Verse:

Book:

Celebrity:

Recipe:

Memory:

Color:

Song:

Movie:

Person:

Animal:

Plant:

Food:

Being a Role Model

I feel that there is a big responsibility that comes with being an artist and having a platform to speak from. I try to lighten the weight by reminding myself that I'm not perfect. I'm going to mess up because I can't do everything right. But I also try to make sure that I don't abuse my role. I need to accept my responsibility and try, with everything in me, to stay focused on Christ Jesus. Then with God's help—and with the help of family and friends—I can lead people toward Christ.

Genuinely Me with God

It's my primary goal to be genuine with God because then I can stay genuine as a Christian artist. I know that more than anything, God wants us to be real with Him, to just let down and be ourselves with Him. I talk to God about my day, about my concerts, and about the teens I meet. If I'm not being real, then my relationship with Him won't be as open. If we willingly open up to Him, our relationship with Him will be closer than we could ever imagine!

Genuine. Adj. Free from
hypocrisy or pretense, sincere,
authentic, not counterfeit or
fraudulent, nor artificial,
without pretense, valid, honest, real

How I'm Genuine in My Life

Genuine

Things that Make Stacie Ialugh...

What little kids say

If I stay up too late, I'll laugh at anything!

My family

Movies from the '80s

When I trip and mess up while dancing on stage and my dancers notice—I look at them, and we crack up.

I laugh at myself a lot!

Aerobic videos

Making home videos with my siblings

I Laugh When...

being
genuine
in
Beauty

I know that life is incredibly
precious, so I try to live it to the fullest.

Who Decides
Who's Beautiful?

Seeing perfect models on TV and in magazines affects how girls think. We see pictures of models in their bathing suits, and then we look in the mirror and say, "I don't look like that." We think our bodies should look just like theirs, and we get caught up in this worldly picture of what we're supposed to look like. It's so overwhelming, and I give in to it often.

I don't like my big nose, my chubby fingers, or the fact that my arms are never toned. Like a lot of girls, I also don't like my thighs, so I hardly ever wear shorts. It's a good thing for me that three-quarter length skirts and capri's are so popular!

Even though there are parts of my body I don't like, I know that genuine beauty comes from knowing Christ. Being genuinely beautiful is just being yourself. God made us all beautiful. He thinks that we're all a priceless treasure.

Who decides who's beautiful and who's not? Society can't, if we don't let it. We need to remember that we're all pieces of art that He's created. He's so proud of us that He says, "Just look at my art."

Eyebrow Disaster

"WINK WINK"

WHILE I WAS ON THE ROAD RECENTLY, I WAS SCHEDULED TO APPEAR ON A TELEVISION PROGRAM IN VIRGINIA. TO GET READY FOR IT, I BOUGHT A HOME WAXING KIT AT THE STORE. I HAD DONE IT MYSELF SEVERAL TIMES BEFORE, SO I THOUGHT IT WOULD BE FINE.

THE DAY BEFORE THE INTERVIEW, I PUT ON THE WAX. WHEN YOU PULL THE WAX OFF, YOUR SKIN IS ALWAYS KIND OF RED, BUT THAT TIME, IT RIPPED MY SKIN OFF! I WAS TAKING SOME ACNE MEDICINE THAT MADE MY SKIN VERY DRY—SO DRY THAT THE WAX TOOK MY SKIN WITH IT. TINY LITTLE DOTS OF BLOOD WERE ON MY EYEBROWS, AND THEN THEY TURNED INTO LITTLE SCABS. IT WAS AWFUL.

FOR THE INTERVIEW, WE CAKED MAKE UP OVER MY SCABS, AND YOU COULDN'T SEE THEM. BUT I COULDN'T REALLY OPEN MY EYES WIDE BECAUSE IT HURT. NOW, WHEN I LOOK AT PICTURES FROM THE INTERVIEW, I CAN REALLY TELL THAT I WAS VERY UNCOMFORTABLE. I COULDN'T DO MANY FACIAL EXPRESSIONS BECAUSE IT WAS SO PAINFUL. EVERYBODY ON THE ROAD WITH ME WAS LAUGHING HYSTERICALLY.

Truth. n. Reality, actuality, consistent with fact or reality; consistent with God's special revelation.

genuine

"WINK WIN

My whole life, I've always wanted—in whatever I was doing—to be different. I always loved the thought of doing something that would stand out, or saying something in a way that was different. As a little girl, when I'd see people trying new things, or anytime I'd hear somebody say something really different, I'd say, "Oh, that's so cool." I never thought I'd be professional musician, but I love it because it fits that side of me that wants to be different.

I once heard a guy speaking who said, "If I asked you, 'Who's Michael Jordan?' You'd say, 'a basketball player.'" Then the speaker said, "But that's not who he is. That's what he does." I thought his point was so amazing.

It's true that I'm a singer. That's what I do, but that's not totally who I am. I don't have to rely on what I do for my self-worth. There's something else that defines me, and that's God. He made me like no one else!

My bedroom is definitely different.
I started out by decorating it in pink and zebra.
I have a zebra comforter, zebra pillows, a lamp with
a zebra lampshade, and a zebra garbage can.
Later, I added in other colors, like this shiny purple-
blue color, and I've thrown in other colors like yellow
and green.

IT'S DIFFERENT!

IT'S ME!

Stacie's Room

I LOVE CLOTHES! DON'T BE AFRAID TO TRY WEARING
NEW STUFF AND BEING DIFFERENT. WHEN YOU WALK INTO A
STORE, DON'T SAY, "OH, I SAW A GIRL
WEARING THIS, SO IT MUST BE COOL."
INSTEAD, LOOK FOR THINGS YOU'VE
NEVER SEEN BEFORE THAT YOU LIKE,
AND TRY IT. IT'S FUN TO BE
CONFIDENT IN BEING YOURSELF.

genuine

POP Quiz

Find Your Fab Feature

1. If you were chosen to be on a reality-TV show and you could only take one thing from your make-up stash, what would it be?

- **A.** Mascara
- **B.** Lipstick/lip gloss
- **C.** Glitter

2. What do your friends love most about you?

A. Your outrageous fashion sense

B. Your absolute honesty

C. Your easy-going nature

3. One of your worst nightmares would be:

A. Finding out your mom read your personal e-mail

B. Catching your crush in a lie

C. Overhearing someone gossiping about your best friend

4. If your life were made into a box-office hit, which actress would win the starring role?

A. Sarah Michelle Gellar

B. Jennifer Lopez

C. Julia Roberts

5. You would rather spend a Saturday night:

A. Catching a chic flick with your girlfriends

B. Talking on the phone with a cute guy

C. Listening to CDs at a friend's house

Genuine

Here's the *scoop* on your best *beauty* feature and what *you* should *do* about it.

If you answered mostly (A)'s, your eyes are your best feature. You have amazing insight. You can spot a friend's problem in a heartbeat, and you usually know just what it takes to make her feel better. Emphasize your eyes by using mascara and liner on your top lids but leaving your bottom lids bare. Become even more beautiful by looking for something good in every person you know.

If you answered mostly (B)'s, accent your lips. Honesty is your best policy. You tell the truth with couth, even when it's not the popular thing to do. Play up those lips with this tip: Use a brush to apply clear gloss first, then brush on a little color to give your lips a berry-stained look. For a genuine glow, remember to also speak up when there's a compliment to pass on, even to the girl who has it in for you.

If you answered mostly (C)'s, bejewel and bedazzle your luscious lobes. That's right, your listening ears set you apart. You're the first person your friends want to call when they need a sounding board. Try hoop earrings when you're feeling bold or sparkling studs for a more subtle mood. And to buff up your inner beauty, look for those who might be feeling lonely or left out, and strike up a conversation. Your listening ears might be just the kindness they need.

being
genuine
with
friends

Do something crazy,
and do it like you mean it!

Making Friends

Since I'm outgoing, it's not hard for me to start a conversation with somebody, but it takes me awhile to build a close friendship.

The most important trait I look for in a friend is trust. I like it when someone really takes the time to get to know me, and when I can get to know them. Building trust takes honesty, and being real with each other is the first step.

With my closest friends, I laugh a lot. I think that's really important in friendships—laughing together!

A close friend is someone you can tell everything to. Most girls dress up for guys, but I think girls do that for other girls too. But for me, I want to feel comfortable in a friendship. I don't think we should feel weird if we hang out in our pajamas together.

I'M ON THE ROAD WITH PEOPLE WHO ARE WONDERFUL.
I travel with my four dancers, who are ages fifteen to
nineteen. What are the chances of five girls all getting
along with each other so well? Probably not great, but we're
all close friends. We didn't know each other before we
started traveling together, but we all happen to have
personalities that click. I know that God has placed each
of them with me because He knew that we could all be
such great friends who care for each other.

My dancers and I shop for outfits together for our shows,
and before a concert, we get ready on the bus together.
To get pumped, we'll play loud dance music. We'll dance
around as we get ready for the show. Then we all pray
together before we go on stage. It's a great way to prepare
ourselves for the audience.

FriEnds
on tHE RoAd

A Painful
Friendship

For a couple of years, I had one friend who was probably the best friend that I had ever had. She just really loved the Lord, and she challenged me a lot spiritually. We also had a lot of fun together, and I often thanked God for such a great friendship.

One summer, I went away for a few months, and by the time I came back, she was totally turned around. She got involved with the wrong crowd and seemed to have lost her faith. It was so weird. Out of everybody in the world, I never expected it from her.

Great friends are hard to find in junior high, so losing her was very tough. I spent a lot of nights crying and praying about it, and I talked to my mom and sister. I wanted to help her and let her know that I loved her, but at the same time, I didn't know what to do. I knew I couldn't do anything to change her—only God could—so I had to let go.

SOMETIMES IT'S EASY TO FORGET
THAT WE HAVE TO STAY UNDER GOD'S PROTECTION.
WE HAVE TO STAY UNDER HIS COVERING. WE CAN'T JUST
ASSUME THAT HE'S GOING TO PROTECT US JUST
BECAUSE WE ARE SAVED. WE HAVE TO CONTINUE PURSUING
AFTER CHRIST. WE HAVE TO STAY IN LOVE WITH HIM
AND RUN HARD AFTER WHAT GOD HAS PLANNED
FOR US TO DO.

When a Friend Hurts You

As a teenager, it's hard to keep things in perspective because so much is going on at one time. It's so easy to get really angry with a friend who does something wrong. Looking back, I realize now how many things I took way too seriously in my friendships.

I've learned that if I step back, I can see how I might have contributed to a bad situation, how I might have hurt my friend too. Now I know that if I have a friend that I want to keep, then I have to be willing to forgive and work through it.

Top 10 Ways to Encourage a Friend

1. Organize a get-together for her.

2. Take her to do something that she loves to do, even if you don't really like to do it, and make it fun just because you are together.

3. Listen.

4. Make her laugh.

5. Compliment her on things that you've really thought about and that you really mean.

6. Be attentive to her feelings.

7. Care about the things she cares about and let her know.

8. Leave notes or messages telling her how awesome she is.

9. Make time for her.

10. Bring her a cup of coffee or some fast food.

Being
genuine
with my
family

Don't let a day pass you by without doing
something that you are proud of.

The Orrico Clan

I have the best family in the world. We're really close. We have a fun time together, and we laugh a lot. Anytime someone asks me, "How do you stay grounded with your music career?" I know it all comes back to my family.

My younger siblings make me feel so loved. Alicia makes up dances to all my songs, and she likes to borrow my clothes. It's so flattering that she wants to be like me. Although Joshua is very competitive and tough, he is also very compassionate. When he comes home from school, he'll give me a hug and say, "I missed you today."

My older brother, Jesse, lives in Nashville, Tennessee, where I live, and he comes over for dinner often. He's also my (awesome!) road manager.

My older sister, Rachel, is my best friend. She lives in Denver, but we still talk several times a week, even if it's just a quick conversation. We check up on each other.

I'm not a crier, and neither is my sister, Rachel. Before she left to move back to Denver, though, I was having a major emotional week, and I'd been crying to her over several things. After she left, she called me and said, "Do you need to cry about anything while we're on the phone? This is your chance!" I love it that she's always there!

Top **5** Ways to Bug Your Siblings

Go jump on their bed at 6 in the morning.

Ask them embarrassing questions in front of their friends.

• **Backwash in their drink.**

Look over their shoulder while they are stressed out doing homework.

Put a song that they hate on repeat.

TiMe to SiT and ChAt
. . . and Do DisHes!

In my family, we've all always tried to be home at the same time for dinner. At the end of the day, when everybody's kind of tired, we all just sit down and relax together and talk about our day. We don't answer the phone, and we don't get up till we're done. Then everybody does dishes together. My little brother, Joshua, sometimes tries to get out of it by saying, "I have to go to the bathroom!" So the rest of us say, "We'll save you some dishes!"

Stacie's Family

Mom: Patti Dad: Dean Older Sister: Rachel Older Brother: Jesse
The Twins—Younger Brother: Joshua Younger Sister: Alicia

genuine

STaciE's Pet PeEves
at HoMe

- Walking across the kitchen with socks on and then stepping in water and having to live with wet socks on your feet.
- When somebody in my family takes something out of the microwave before the timer has gone off and they don't press cancel. Then I look up at the microwave to see what time it is, and it says twelve seconds.
- I am sort of claustrophobic, so it drives me crazy when I am in a car or small room and my younger siblings are yelling and wrestling next to me. LET ME OUT!
- I really don't like it when people spit toothpaste into my sink and don't rinse it out.
- Trying to spread hard butter on bread.

MY Pet PeEves!

A Family of Faith

Faith is important to my family. We go to church together as much as possible. We also pray together quite a lot.

Recently, my grandparents came into town, and the whole family prayed together. We prayed especially for my little cousin who is sick with leukemia. It was so comforting to be able to talk to God about it together.

My family also encourages each other spiritually. My parents, and especially my older brother, Jesse, will ask me, "So, how are your devotions going? What are you learning?" In our family, we talk about our relationships with God openly.

It seems that in some families, faith can be treated like a secret, or some teens don't want their parents to ask about their faith or their devotions. But I really appreciate it.

My mom spends time with God every morning, and sometimes she'll tell me about it. Or she'll write down little thoughts or Bible verses on a piece of paper, and then she will give it to me and say, "This was so sweet, so I wrote it down for you."

How Stacie Became a Christian

My parents were both Christians when they got married, so I was born into a family of strong believers. When I was about three and a half years old, I was sitting on the floor playing with my Barbies. Then my sister, who is three years older than I am, came in and sat down. She asked me if I loved Jesus, and I said, "Yeah!" Then she asked me if I had ever prayed and asked Him to come into my heart, and I said no. So she prayed with me that day.

Dress-up at Grandma's

Growing up in Seattle, Washington, my mom's parents were only five hours away, so we'd visit with them pretty often. Through them, I've learned what it means when the Bible talks about blessings being passed down—how God loves to take the fruit of one generation and pass it down to the next. They love the Lord so much.

One of the best memories I have is playing dress-up in their old, huge Victorian house. In the basement, my grandma has stored all of her clothes from the 1930s to 1970s. She even has her wedding dress. My brothers and sisters and I would have a blast trying on her clothes, hats, shoes, and jewelry.

My grandpa, who is hilarious, would come down and put on funny socks and pull them up real high and then put on sandals over them. He'd put on sweats and pull the pants way up. Then he'd put on a funny hat and funny glasses, and he'd say, "Stacie, I'm gonna take you to school today!" I'd laugh and yell, "No!"

genuine

43

Top 10 Ways to Eat a Bowl of Cheerios

1) Without a spoon

2) With a straw

3) Just stick your face right in it

4) Without milk

5) Wait until it's soggy

6) With an ice cream scoop

7) Pour your milk in the box and eat it straight out

8) Try using cream or half-and-half instead of milk. It is really good. I know from experience.

9) One Cheerio at a time

10) Close your eyes, pick it up and drink it, and try not to swallow any cereal.

Being genuine with Guys

Be content to be alone, and accept each
blessing of being with someone you love.

WhEn ShouLd you Date?

Some people have asked me the right age to begin dating, but I don't think there is a set age. It can be different for different people. Some girls are ready to date when they're younger, and other girls are ready later.

I think that a great relationship starts with you. It's important to feel really comfortable with yourself and with being by yourself. Then when you meet a guy and you start going out, it'll be awesome.

I've gone out with guys in groups (which is what my parents like!), and I've also gone out a few times alone with a guy. I am careful, though, not to just go on a date with anyone who asks me. If I'm not really interested, then I don't go. I feel like every time a girl goes out with somebody, she leaves a little piece of herself with him. The memories and the emotions are left behind. I don't believe in just throwing myself into dating a bunch of different guys. I want my heart to be complete for my future husband.

I'M NOT **THAT** INTO A GUY'S PHYSICAL APPEARANCE. SOMETIMES, THE **REALLY** HOT GUYS **HAVE** REALLY LAME PERSONALITIES. AND OFTEN, IF A GUY HAS A REALLY **GREAT** PERSONALITY, IT JUST MAKES **HIM** SO INCREDIBLY HOT!

My Future Husband

I probably think about my future husband more than anybody in the whole world!

I want to marry a guy who understands the music industry, but I also want him to have his own career. Because being an artist can seem like such an important job, I want his job to be a big job, too. He doesn't have to make a lot of money, but I want him to have his own distinction.

I don't want to feel like I'm dominating the family. I don't want a guy who kisses my feet. I'm independent, but I think that a lot of women want to be so independent that they don't want to feel like their husband is higher than they are. That's not me. I want him to be in charge.

47

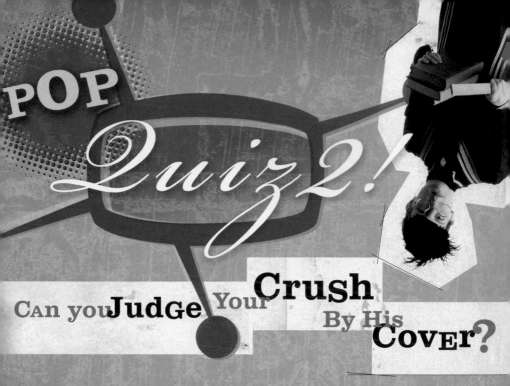

POP *Quiz 2!*

Can you **Judge** Your **Crush** By His **Cover?**

Super Prep: Your crush is a clean-cut cutie—at least all the cheerleaders think so. He'd rather walk on hot coals than walk out of the house with his polo wrinkled. He digs chics he can take to the symphony or a football game. If you're his date, be ready for either one!

Nature Boy: This guy is a tree-huggin' hottie, and he needs a girl who cares about the world. He'd rather adopt a highway than toss his trash onto one. He likes outdoor concerts and hangin' with his friends. Lay low if you wanna catch this fish. He's into girls with lots of confidence and very little cling.

Baseball Cap

```
Baseball Cap
       Yes /          \ No
          /            \
    Khakis  <-- Sometimes -->  Birkenstocks
```

Khakis:
- Always → Polo Shirt
- Never → Tie Dye
- Occasionally → Glasses

Birkenstocks:
- Always → Tie Dye
- Never → Glasses
- Just for Laughs → Dyed hair

Polo Shirt	Tie Dye	Glasses	Dyed hair
Super Prep	**Nature Boy**	**Brainiac**	**Class Clown**

Brainiac: Break out the books for this study date, but be on guard. This straight-laced babe-magnet might make you see stars by quoting Shakespeare's best love scenes. He's going places, and he wants a girl who is, too. His date picks are foreign films, walks in the park, and intellectual conversations over mochaccinos or lattés.

Class Clown: Everybody loves to have this guy around, so be prepared to take a number. This loveable lunatic needs a girl who's happy to let him be on center-stage. He'll do almost anything for a laugh, so expect the unexpected when you're with him. His date picks are funny flicks and anything that involves a crowd.

I don't think I've
ever really been in
love, but I believe
that true love is that
perfect mix of best
friendship and total
romance together.
I think if you have
just one by itself,
then you'll miss out.

Being
Genuine
in
My faith

He loves you for who you
are now and who you will be . . .
from the song "Genuine"

I have a devotional time every night before I go to bed. I can't go to sleep until I do it. Right now, I am reading My Utmost for His Highest by Oswald Chambers, and in my devotional journal, I write about what God is teaching me through the book I'm reading.

I also keep a prayer journal. Sometimes when Christians talk or pray to God, we'll talk so spiritually, with words that we don't truly understand, instead of just talking to Him in every-day language. In my prayer journal, I write to God in letter form, just telling Him about my day like I am talking to my best friend. I also write down all of my prayer requests under different sections like friends, family, career, and so on.

Every day, I also pick one character trait of God, and at night, I write about how He's shown that part of Himself to me. For example, if I've had a very restless day, then I'll write how God has shown me His peace.

Then I'll pray over it,

thanking Him for Who He is.

Stacie

I am thankful for—
all the amazing opportunities that
I've had this year.
That God has protected me through
so many crazy things. I know
that he has probably saved me from
more then I know.
The love that has stayed in our
family and household through all
the change.
That once again we have new people
to meet and places to see and things
to look forward to.

I Can Do It By Myself!
(Or Not)

I don't like to let people do stuff for me. I want to do things for myself. Sometimes, my mom will know something about my schedule or plans before I do, and it will bother me. Then she reminds me, "I'm your mother—I'm going to know all this stuff anyway!"

I also don't like to let other people help me when I'm on the road, so my manager, Britt Ham, or my mom will say, "Stacie, chill. We're gonna help you. Everybody's going to do this together."

God has really been working on me about my self-reliance. Even with God, I'll sometimes say, "I can make it through this by myself," and I'll forget to let Him be in charge of my life. It's funny because even though God stays right beside me through everything, if I tell Him I want to try and do it by myself, He'll let me try. It's my choice. But then, I'll lay awake at night for hours thinking about stuff until I finally pray, "Okay, God. I changed my mind. I need your help." And He's just waiting with open arms to help me.

peaceful
Places

- There is no other place in the world where I am as peaceful and thoughtful as on the beach. I really love being at the ocean and being with God while I'm sitting on the sand.

- Sometimes it just feels so much easier to talk to God when you're sitting outside, looking at the sky, surrounded by pretty trees.

- At our house, our yard rises up on this hill, and at the top, we have a bench that looks over all the hills. You can see everything from up there. It's so awesome. It's a special place for me to talk with God.

My Special PlacEs with GoD

genuine

54

Sharing *My Faith*

I think different people are called to share Christ in different ways. Some people are good at evangelism, at preaching the gospel straight out. Some people talk about heaven and hell, and other people are good at handing out Bibles and tracts. I like to take a relationship approach. I like to take the time to build a friendship with trust. Then, you both can feel comfortable talking about personal things—and then I can share Christ with them.

A lot of people, especially teenagers, just feel like they're living fine without Jesus, and they don't understand why they need to make a change in their lives. They need somebody they trust and know to explain it!

Hopefully, even if I'm not the one who tells them the whole gospel story, I'm at least **"planting seeds."** If I can get people thinking about faith in Christ and asking questions, then I feel like that's part of the whole process of coming to know our Savior.

continued . . .

Little seeds can make such a huge impact, like seeking out non-Christians, making time to spend with them, getting to know them with love, and asking if you can pray for them. My grandpa once told me that he met with a guy only three times, and then the guy accepted the Lord. Soon after, the guy died from cancer.

People without Christ can be so insecure, but Christians can be confident because Jesus is our support. We can let God's truth shine through everything we do, even if it's just smiling at someone, or being nice to the person behind the counter.

"Know that the Lord is God. He made us,

and we belong to him. we are his people,

the sheep he tends."

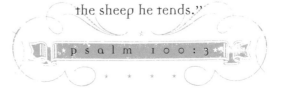

psalm 100:3

Being
Genuine
when facing
peer pressure

There is something wonderful
about going somewhere just the way
you are and being comfortable with it.

SHopping for the Right Me

In junior high, I was surrounded by classmates who were making bad decisions, and it wasn't appealing to me at all. I started hanging out with an older group. I wanted to be accepted, but since they were into the party scene, I felt more pressure than I did in my other peer group. Everybody was drinking, and all the couples would just make out the whole time. It was **supposed** to be fun, but anytime I got too physical with a guy, it made me feel yuck.

I was doing things I never thought I would, and I just felt dumb and gross. It was a learning experience I came out of saying, "I know I don't want to do that. I know I don't want to go there again." I was trying too hard to fit in. I wasn't being genuine with myself.

When it comes to dealing with peer pressure, my philosophy is that I have to make my decisions beforehand about what I will and won't do. We can set our standards ahead of time. Then, when we're faced with a tough choice, there won't be any question about how to answer, and we won't get caught in the moment!

EVERYBODY GOES THROUGH TIMES WHEN THEY FEEL PEER PRESSURE ABOUT SOME THINGS. WE SOMETIMES GIVE IN TO IT IF WE'RE TRYING TO FIT IN. IT'S LIKE GOING SHOPPING, TRYING DIFFERENT STUFF ON. WE WANT TO SEE WHAT APPEALS TO US, AND TO OTHER PEOPLE, BUT IF WE COMPROMISE OUR FAITH, WE'LL JUST BE LOST.

StAcie Digs These Activities

I'M NOT THE CAMPING TYPE, BUT I LOVE TO DO THINGS OUTSIDE, LIKE GOING TO PARKS AND PLAYING FOOTBALL. I ALSO LOVE DOING GIRLY STUFF—MANICURES, PEDICURES, FACIALS. MY FAVORITE THING EVER IS WATCHING OLD MOVIES. WHEN I'M IN AN OVERLY DRAMATIC MOOD, I LOVE CARY GRANT MOVIES.

MOVIE Classics

A Pressure-Packed
Photo Shoot

Modesty is important to me when I'm picking out clothes for concerts, photo shoots, and videos. When I choose the outfits ahead of time, there isn't any question about whether it's too revealing or too tight.

One time, though, I felt pressured to wear clothes I wasn't comfortable wearing. I went to a photo shoot by myself and when I arrived, I found that clothes had been picked out for me. Some of it was just too small and some of it was just not me.

I considered just going home, but some adults kept saying, "Just try it. If the pictures come back and you don't like them, you don't have to use them." So I gave in. I ended up wearing these pants that were just so way-too-tight, and this shirt that was cut too low. It just wasn't me. I felt so nasty all day, and I couldn't believe I was wearing it. We spent a lot of money on a shoot for photos we never used. I learned a lesson in setting limits ahead of time and speaking out about my decision.

genuinely Unique

God created His people with so many different talents. We're each a unique member of the body of Christ. But if we're too busy trying to be someone else, then we can miss out on what God called us to do. We'll never fulfill His plan for our lives. We need to focus on what He created us to be, not on what others say or think about us.

DreAdEd Gossip

As a Christian artist, I sometimes deal with gossip that tries to make me out to be something I'm not. For example, a couple of articles have been written about me where what I've said has been taken out of context. They'll try to make me sound like a snot, or like I'm being rude about something, or like I'm competitive with other Christian artists. Those kinds of things are so disappointing, but I tell myself not to be upset, not to worry that people will believe those things. I just have to say, "I know what I meant by that. And God knows what I meant by that. And that's all that matters."

Unfortunately, many people are going to believe that I meant something else, but I just have to be secure in knowing that my heart is seeking God. If I am focused on God, then I can't focus on what other people say or think about me.

GOSSIP CAN RUIN RELATIONSHIPS AND FRIENDSHIPS, AND IT CRITICIZES SOMEONE THAT GOD SO CAREFULLY AND LOVINGLY CREATED.

Focus on School!

When my singing schedule started getting too busy, it was very stressful for me to keep up with school. I would have failed because I was gone for months at a time, so I started homeschooling.

While I'm traveling, I take my studies with me. Since I don't have a scheduled class time, I do my schoolwork around the different activities on the road. Then I can be available for all of the decisions we make. Also, if I have five songs in my head, I can write them down right away instead of waiting until class is over!

BUT IT'S EASY TO GET SIDETRACKED FROM MY STUDIES BY ALL OF THE PRESSURES AND ACTIVITIES OF MY SINGING. That's why I'm glad that my tutor understands that my time is crazy, and that she also helps me apply my studies to my music.

We spend a lot of time in literature, vocabulary,

continued . . .

and reading because it relates to my songwriting and speaking in public.

Most people go to school to prepare for a career, but I'm already in my career. My motivation for school is different. Learning new things is fun as well as important to me. I want to finish high school because I know that if God chooses, my job as a professional musician could pass away. I want to be ready to act whenever He calls, so my focus is on Him.

What I want to be When I Grow Up

Before I became a Christian artist, I wanted to be an FBI agent, an interior decorator, a wedding coordinator, and a brain surgeon. I never even had "professional musician" on my list!

extreme for jesus

Being a true follower of Jesus and radically turning your life over to him, that's what being Extreme for Jesus™ is all about. It's a challenge to live for Jesus totally, whatever the cost.